How To Manage Your Money

Guide To Personal Finance Budgeting And Management: Step-By-Step Plan For Money Budgeting And Management Today Strategies For Budgeting, Planning, And Managing Finances To Attain Wealth And Eliminate Debt

Albin Leitner

Impulsive Purchases and Immediate Satisfaction.

Impulsive purchase and quick pleasure are closely related ideas that often occur simultaneously and substantially impact consumer behaviour and spending patterns. Purchasing goods or services without giving them careful thought or assessment is referred to as "impulse buying." Irrational cravings and impulses drive it, many sparked by the promise of instant gratification.

On the other hand, moment delight refers to the sense of fulfilment or satisfaction that comes from quickly receiving or using something desired. The desire for an absolute thrill or reward, eschewing the postponement or delay of gratification, often accompanies more astute dynamic cycles.

Moment satisfaction and motivation purchasing are becoming increasingly popular due to the ascent of customer culture, showcasing approaches, and the openness of online shopping. Retailers strategically design their spaces and businesses to attract clients and create an environment that encourages risky purchases. Several tactics are employed to leverage impulsive purchasing habits, such as time-sensitive promotions, flash deals, and eye-catching merchandise close to checkout stations.

Moment satisfaction and motivated purchase may have multiple underlying causes that are localized. Typical components consist of:

1. Emotionally driven decisions: Impulsive purchases are frequently motivated by sentiments rather than a logical analysis of needs or long-term effects. Emotions like passion, desire, stress, and exhaustion can trigger impolite behaviours. Because they know this, marketers craft compelling advertising

campaigns that influence consumers' emotions and appeal to their desires and goals.

2. FOMO: Hasty purchases can be motivated by the fear of missing out on a limited-edition item or a limited-time offer. Social media platforms enhance FOMO by showing other people's experiences and purchases, which makes users feel pressed for time and pressure to keep up with their peers.

3. Moment delight as a mental health booster: Acquiring anything new can immediately make you feel good, improve your mood momentarily, and serve as a reward or emotional retreat. Offering a momentary reprieve from tension, worry, or discontent fosters a sense of contentment or happiness in the here and now.

4. Absence of discretion: Impulsive purchases might sometimes result from a lack of self-discipline or insufficient impulse control. It usually happens when people give in to their

short-term cravings without considering their long-term financial goals or the possible repercussions of impulsive purchases.

It takes self-awareness, self-control, and techniques to offset the emotional motivators to overcome impulsive purchases and develop better spending practices. Here are a few strategies to take into consideration:

1. Create a budget and financial goals that align with your long-term goals. Knowing one's financial objectives and limitations can replace impulsive spending with more thoughtful, value-driven expenditure.

2. Develop delayed gratification: Adopt a delayed gratification mindset instead of caving into immediate desires. Interrupt and give yourself time to consider the purchase, evaluating its necessity and fit with your traits and goals. Delaying purchases allows for more rational, independent guidance and reduces careless behaviour.

3. Consider close-to-home triggers: Attention to the close-to-home cues that encourage buying. Exist any certain situations, emotions, or sentiments that are more likely than not going to encourage impolite behaviour? Identification of these triggers can help design strategies to counteract them. For instance, they may search for extracurricular activities to fulfil obligations near home or ask friends or family for assistance while feeling pressured to make rash purchases.

4. Mindful spending: Practice mindfulness when deciding what to buy. "Do I need this?" and similar questions should be asked of yourself. or additional "Will this purchase bring happiness or value in the long run?" If you are mindful of how you spend your money, you may avoid rash purchases and make more considered decisions.

5. Minimize susceptibility to enticement: Lessen your contact with situations and

settings that promote rash purchases. Unsubscribe from promotional emails, avoid aimless window shopping and online store browsing, and be mindful of marketing tactics that incite want or urgency.

Understanding the emotional drivers of impulse buys and rapid pleasure might help people recover control over their spending patterns and make better value-based decisions. It involves balancing living in the moment and modifying spending to meet long-term financial goals and personal aspirations.

Collaborative budgeting has been employed successfully by many businesses. However, it is not always effective. Research has indicated that involvement in budget planning does not, in many organizations, increase staff members' motivation to meet assigned goals. Employee attitudes, the company's size and structure, and management's leadership style all influence how well participation goes. Not every financial planning issue can be resolved by participation. That is one way to achieve better results in companies that are receptive to the collaborative concept.

A word of advice: Don't assume that you'll have the same amount left over every month. There can be extra costs if, for example, you're preparing for a vacation or the holidays.

A 50/30/20 Budget Approach: What Is It?

Adhering to a fiscal plan can be advantageous. Sen. Elizabeth Warren initially developed the 50/30/20 paradigm, which is widely used. To put it simply, you.

"Needs" include rent, power, consumables, and the minimum amount required on credit cards. Subscriptions, eating out, and other non-essentials are examples of "wants."

Another useful tool for getting your expenditure in line with your goals is the 50/30/20 rule. If your monthly expenditure on "wants" exceeds thirty per cent of your earnings, assess areas where you may make savings.

Step Four: Create a Checking Account Buffer

Consider setting up a buffer in your checking account if you can. Leave part of your extra cash in checking instead of using it all up or moving it to your savings account. Then, put it all behind you. Fight the urge to waste it by acting like it doesn't exist.

Think of it as a backup plan "just in case." Maintaining a small amount of excess funds in the account may assist you in avoiding overdrawing.

Certain financial organizations, such as Capital One, have eliminated overdraft fees. If your bank is different, those extra costs may pile up.

You can have peace of mind with a cushion. And once you have one, you can focus on moving closer to your retirement or debt reduction goals.

Step 5: Increase Your Funds

You may want to use any extra cash to establish reserves if you feel more in control of your debt and have some buffer in your checking account.

Keep track of your progress as you accumulate savings and pay off debt. That might serve as inspiration to make wise choices, such as increasing investments or cutting expenses.

How Can Someone Who Is New to Savings Start?

The following principles can help you start and grow your savings:

Compare different savings accounts. Savings accounts often offer a small amount of interest as a return on your investment. However, interest rates could vary from one account to the next.

Particularly as your investments rise.

Invest any extra money you make in your investments. Money from a side business, tax returns, employment incentives, and gifts are examples of extra revenue. The extra cash can significantly advance your growth.

Automate the storage process. Reducing your spending can be the most difficult step in increasing your income. An automated savings plan might lessen the pain before you see it in your bank account.

Resist the urge to spend excessively. You might wish to resist the temptation to spend money on items you need rather than the things you want. You can put even more money toward your earnings in this way.

Promotion and Marketing

Formulating a Marketing Plan: The Key to Gastronomic Recognition

Creating a winning recipe with all the necessary components to draw in and keep customers is similar to creating a marketing plan. Similar to how a chef blends different ingredients to produce a harmonious dish, your marketing plan should incorporate strategies highlighting your truck's distinctive features and target customers, such as offline events and internet advertising.

Making Use of Social Media Marketing: The Digital Sizzle Art

Social media is the sizzle that brings people to your food truck in today's connected society. Social media marketing is similar to adding spices to food to enhance its flavour and scent—platforms such as Twitter, Facebook, and Instagram. Post gorgeous images of your food, exclusive behind-the-scenes glimpses, and interesting content that captures the essence of your brand. Curate your social media feed to pique your audience's visual appetites, just like a chef might when garnishing a dish for aesthetic appeal.

Taking Part in Food Truck Festivals and Events: Embracing the Gastronomic Festival

Think of your food truck as a part of an epicurean festival. A food truck festival or event is similar to having a featured chef at a busy food market. These events are a great way to meet other food truck entrepreneurs, get exposure, and present your cuisine to various consumers. In the same way, a chef prepares special delicacies for a festival and offers eventgoers an unforgettable experience that will stick in their minds long after the event.

Partnerships and Cross-Promotions: The Tastes of Concurrent Development

Collaborations in the culinary arts result in innovative and delicious dishes. Similarly, partnerships and cross-promotions might open new business avenues for your food truck. Consider collaborating on collaborative promotions with other nearby companies, such as a coffee shop, brewery, or dessert shop. It's akin to preparing a tasting menu that combines the finest aspects of both cultures. Partnerships broaden the audience for your truck and inject some enthusiasm into what you have to offer.

Gathering and Applying User Input: A Crucial Component of Ongoing Enhancement

Customer feedback is important for your food truck to improve its products, just as a chef uses it to improve their recipes. Use polls, internet reviews, or even informal talks to get feedback. Examine the comments to find areas that could be used better, then make the necessary adjustments. Adjust your food truck's menu according to what your patrons enjoy and recommend, much as a chef would adjust a recipe after conducting taste testing.

You are laying out a plan for the exposure and expansion of your food truck when you create a marketing strategy. You're seasoning your online presence with social media marketing to attract eager consumers. Attending food truck festivals and events is similar to putting on a stage display for your culinary skills. Cross-promotions and collaborations are similar to mixing ingredients to make a pleasant meal. Furthermore, gathering and utilizing consumer feedback is similar to fine-tuning your recipes according to the thoughts of individuals who enjoy them. When your food truck ventures into the marketing realm, it offers more than simply food—it offers relationships, experiences, and a flavorful trip that goes well beyond the truck's boundaries.

Over-engagement

Taking on more duties, obligations, or commitments than you can practically manage in a specific amount of time is called overcommitting. It may result in fatigue, tension, low productivity, and the inability to fulfil deadlines. Observe these pointers to prevent overcommitting:

Evaluate the workload you are now handling: Examine your current obligations, duties, and responsibilities. Think about the time and work involved in each one and assess your ability to take on more responsibilities without sacrificing the calibre of your job or your health.

Make your obligations a priority: Decide which are most important and align with your values and aspirations. Sort them according to urgency and significance. This will enable you to choose which commitments to accept and turn down with knowledge.

Acquire the ability to refuse:

Recognize that when you're already overwhelmed, turning down more commitment offers is acceptable.

Be forceful and graciously turn down offers that don't fit your priorities or would put you beyond your limit.

Remember that turning down something allows you to accept something more significant.

Analyze the bandwidth you have available. When contemplating additional commitments, take into account your time, energy, and resources that are accessible. Be realistic about what you can manage successfully without compromising the quality of your work or your well-being. Establish boundaries based on your awareness of your limitations.

Think about the long-term effects: Think about the possible repercussions of taking on too much. Will it impact your relationships, general performance, or health? Considering the whole picture might help you decide with greater knowledge whether to accept or reject new commitments.

Delegate and work together: If you're experiencing stress, consider assigning responsibilities to others or asking friends, teammates, or coworkers for assistance. You can lessen your workload and ensure that jobs are finished quickly by having people share the responsibility.

Effective communication: If you are already overcommitting, speak candidly and openly with the appropriate parties. Describe your burden and review possible fixes, including moving things around, changing deadlines, or rearranging priority.

Regularly review your schedule:

Spend some time going over your obligations from time to time.

Determine whether any rearranging or reordering of priorities is required to keep a healthy balance.

Have the flexibility to reassess and adjust to ensure you're not taking on too much.

Take care of yourself: Prioritise self-care to maintain physical and emotional health. Make time for relaxation, engage in things revitalizing you, and take breaks. Taking care of yourself not only makes it easier for you to fulfil obligations, but it also helps you avoid burnout. It's crucial to carefully manage your obligations to preserve a positive work-life balance and stay out of overwhelm. You can ensure you have the time and energy to honour your commitments and put your well-being first by being aware of your capacity and choosing carefully what you take.

Delaying

The act of delaying or postponing necessary tasks—often in favour of more enjoyable or less taxing activities—is known as procrastination. Although it's a typical problem for many people, it can seriously impair productivity and lead to needless stress. The following are some methods for overcoming procrastination:

Recognize the causes: Consider your propensity toward procrastination. Is it because you feel overwhelmed, uninterested, or afraid of failing? Identifying the root reasons will enable you to provide focused solutions.

Divide the work into smaller steps: Big jobs can be frightening and daunting, making putting them off easier. Divide them into more manageable, smaller steps. With this method, the task doesn't seem as overwhelming, and you can concentrate on taking things one step at a time.

Give precise timeframes and goals: Establish precise timelines for each activity and specify what has to be done. A well-defined goal and schedule instil a sense of urgency and aid in task prioritization.

Apply productivity strategies: Investigate other productivity strategies, such as the Pomodoro Technique, which calls for working for a predetermined amount of time—for example, 25 minutes—and then taking a little break by dividing your task into manageable chunks.

Get rid of distractions: Determine which distractions are present in your surroundings and get rid of them. Close tabs on your browser, put your phone aside and set up a quiet, dedicated workstation to reduce distractions.

Seek inspiration: Find out what drives you, then make the most of it. Develop self-discipline: Teach yourself to fight the impulse to procrastinate. Procrastination may be fought by connecting to your motivation, whether by finding significance in your job or providing rewards for finishing tasks. Start by setting aside a certain daily period to work only on your assignments. To develop a disciplined work habit, gradually extend the time while remaining consistent.

Seek support and accountability: Talk to a mentor, trustworthy friend, or coworker about your objectives and progress so they can hold you accountable. Your dedication to beating procrastination can grow if you have someone to check in with and offer encouragement.

Control your perfectionism: When you wait for the "perfect" circumstances or worry that you won't live up to your high expectations, perfectionism can frequently result in procrastination. Acknowledge that not everything must be perfect and put more emphasis on progress than perfection.

By engaging in self-care. Ensure you handle stress, eat, sleep, and exercise frequently. It's simpler to remain motivated and concentrated when you feel balanced and invigorated.

It takes self-awareness, discipline, and persistent work to overcome procrastination. You may effectively control procrastination and boost your productivity by practising these strategies and creating wholesome habits.

Method 2: Creating Your Individuality

Steer clear of living for other people.

Your life should be lived for you, not for the benefit of other people. You will never be able to please everyone, so either give up trying or have irrational hopes that you will always be able to please everyone.

The best thing you can do is try to live a happy life according to your moral principles. Above all, when you prioritize pleasing yourself over pleasing others, you will experience your highest self-worth.

If the secret to being happy is having lots of friends, then act in a way that makes other people want to be your friends by being nice and creating beautiful things.

Avoid getting into trouble or dressed badly in an attempt to gain friends. Individuals who surround you with these intentions aren't your friends and will ultimately harm you in the long run.

2. Establish a look and feel.

Don't attempt to be someone else; just be yourself. Discover your sense of style instead of following the crowd and wearing every trendy brand. Your sense of style will help you stand out and boost your confidence, self-esteem, and sense of worth.

Make sure the things you wear and how you wear them speak more about you than anything else.

3. Consider your areas of interest.

Examine what you are interested in or enthusiastic about to learn more about who you are and what you appreciate best about yourself.

❖ Do you think learning to play chess could make you smarter, more confident, and more confident in yourself? Discover it.

❖ Have you ever wished you were a dancer? Next, execute it.

You are the only one preventing yourself from engaging in your hobbies. You can join clubs at your school to try out new activities, artistic interests, athletic endeavours, and other things that interest you.

4. Look for individuals that you truly click with.

Being surrounded by great friends is the finest defence against life's more challenging elements. A true friend always brings your inherent delight and grandeur to your attention.

Surround yourself with people who like and respect you for who you are if you want to maintain your self-worth and self-esteem. Good companions should share a lot of your interests and aspirations in life.

It will strengthen your bond and enable you to encourage one another. It's acceptable, though, if not all of your pals are interested in the same things you are. Some disparities are good because they make you consider different viewpoints and ideas.

Refrain from interacting with those that bring you down. Someone is not truly your friend if they make your life worse. You should break up with someone if they make you feel horrible about yourself or pressure you into doing anything wrong. Our friends shouldn't be able to bring us down.

5. Show courage and assurance. Avoid letting other people control you.

Refrain from giving in to external pressure. Prioritizing your wants and being loyal to who you are, even while striving to make other people happy and refraining from being selfish, is important.

The courage to stand up for what's right for you can profoundly affect your self-esteem and personality. Share your thoughts with friends and other students when you interact with them.

Request the things you require. Say "no," if it's necessary or desired. Probably most importantly, don't feel bad about doing these things.

Gaining Respect for Oneself

1. Maintain proper hygiene.

Maintaining your cleanliness is one way you can boost your self-esteem. You may increase your self-awareness by looking after yourself.

You need to maintain good hygiene if you want to look after yourself. Wash your hair and skin frequently. Cleanse your hair and teeth. Put on some deodorant. You'll feel better about your physical appearance as a result of this.

Personal hygiene products can frequently be obtained for free from various community sources. Local churches and organizations offer numerous services that provide basic needs.

2. Don a neat, well-fitting clothing.

Don't forget to keep your clothes clean. When dirty, wash and fold to avoid wrinkles. Steer clear of clothing that has multiple tears or holes in it.

If the stain cannot be removed, discard the affected clothing. Don clothing that is too small or loose; instead, wear clothing that fits.

Numerous neighbourhood and community outreach organizations offer free clothing if you have financial difficulties buying new clothes.

Secondhand businesses also tend to have far lower prices for clothing than other retail establishments. Check out secondhand stores if you're worried that the only apparel you can find must be updated.

You'll have the best chances if you shop at stores near large educational institutions. There's a greater likelihood that you'll find almost new and calibrated clothing that will last for many years.

3. Give yourself some time to unwind.

Adolescence is critical, and teenagers frequently don't get enough sleep. Even if you may believe that sleeping less is OK, it is detrimental to your health.

Researchers have shown a correlation between poor sleep quality and reduced levels of optimism and self-esteem. Getting at least 8 or 9 hours of sleep per night is easy advice to help high school students feel more confident.

4. Work out

Exercise has a big role in making you feel comfortable in your skin. If you are overweight or generally unfit, you may experience fatigue, shortness of breath, or self-consciousness.

You'll feel better and have more energy after working out. Your heart rate for ten minutes or more. Exercise with running, squats, and push-ups, or take a stroll. Anything that works for you is acceptable if you are consistent and persistent.

5. Consume food sensibly.

Eating well will boost your self-esteem, just like exercise does. Too many bad meals will make you feel sluggish, bloated, and sick.

Eating well will increase your energy and make you happier. You'll be able to feel better about yourself due to feeling better.

Retirement Investment Vehicles

You have financial options similar to the various institutions available to accomplish your retirement objective. Investing options include equities, bonds, real estate, exchange-traded funds, and platforms for lending. Your objectives, risk tolerance, and potential profits should all influence your decision-making. The following are a few cars to think about:

The 500 Standard & Poor's Index

When the Standard & Poor's 500 (S&P 500) index was first introduced in 1923, it comprised 233 firms. Based on their market capitalization—the sum of a company's shares and share price—the S&P 500 evaluates the performance of the leading publicly traded firms in the United States. From 1957 until December 2022, it adopted 500 enterprises and returned 10.15 per cent (Maverick, 2023).

The S&P 500 index cannot be directly invested in, but shares in ETFs that reflect its performance can be purchased. The benefit is that these funds offer immediate diversification to reduce risk and are frequently less expensive than purchasing individual stocks. In an inflation-adjusted fund that replicates the performance of the S&P 500, how long would it take you to attain your retirement target?

Assume for this discussion that your retirement funds are $10,000 and your goal is $1 million. Additionally, suppose that you make a $12,000 yearly contribution, receive an AIR of 10%, and experience 6% personal inflation. This indicates that, after accounting for inflation, the real return is 4% (10% − 6% = 4%). To retire, 37 years will pass. You will retire three years short of turning sixty if you are currently twenty years old, which is probably not what you want.

Remember that your retirement savings will exceed $1 million because inflation will have driven up the value. Still, that will equal $1 million in modern currency.

Actual Property

How quickly could you retire if you invested in rental real estate rather than just funds that track the S&P 500? Recognize that monthly cash flow from your rental property investment should be reinvested. Rental property investments are similar to dividend-paying stock investments.

Investing in equities only costs a few dollars per share, but purchasing rental real estate demands a significant financial commitment. However, renting real estate can be a hedge against inflation if you can understand risk-reduction techniques and clever real estate financing. Rental real estate has produced an average yearly return of 4.18% since 1928. The real return is -1.82% annually at your 6% annual inflation rate (Steiner, 2023). Therefore, if you start with $10,000 and contribute $12,000 a year, you will not have the $1 million in today's worth at retirement that you had been hoping for. Purchasing rental property alone won't allow you to retire early. This is the cost of making investments in secure financial instruments!

Platforms for Crowdfunding Real Estate

Investing through a real estate crowdfunding platform is an alternative to direct investments. This real estate investment entity is still a relatively new endeavour. Money from investors is gathered through real estate crowdfunding and put into a pool to buy properties. This is a fantastic method to get a sizable amount of cash upfront for a real estate property while reducing danger.

Find a platform that promotes investment properties if you want to participate in real estate crowdfunding. Then, after considering the costs, minimum investment requirements, and previous investor distributions, pick a property that you believe would yield the desired returns at a manageable degree of risk. Select a crowdsourcing site that accepts unsophisticated or non-accredited investors. If your property is profitable, you may receive returns ranging from 2% to 20% (Folger, 2023).

The secret to successful real estate crowdfunding is locating a reliable platform. Nobody wants to part up their hard-earned money to fund a fraud.

You can retire in roughly 33 years if you invest in a crowdfunding property using the strategy detailed in the S&P 500 section and get a 5% actual return. This implies that if you begin saving for retirement at 20, you can likely retire well before 60.

Lending Sites

Traditionally, you would apply at a bank or credit union to borrow money. You can be subject to high-interest rates if your credit score isn't very good. Peer-to-peer lending has been an option since 2005 as an alternative to borrowing from traditional financial institutions. Under this arrangement, an individual borrows money from a third party known as an investor.

Peer-to-peer lending may need collateral, just like traditional lending, depending on whether you're asking for an unsecured or secured loan. Collateral is required for secured loans but not for unsecured ones.

The first step in investing in peer-to-peer lending is to create an account on a reliable platform and deposit money for loans. Some platforms let you diversify by dividing the amount you deposit into many amounts that you can loan out. The returns you receive might range from 7% to 48%, depending on the platform (Ruseva, 2022). Like banks, investors stand to lose money if a borrower defaults, which explains the potential for large returns.

Let's say you discover a regulated lending platform with an average yearly return of 15%. You make the same kind of investment as in the cases above. You'll retire in twenty-five years and around nine months, with a real AIR of 9%. This can be a terrific investment method and help you accomplish your $1 million retirement target while still young if you can afford the risk.

Five Strategies for Managing Real Estate Client Expectations

Have you ever had a breakdown in communication with a client? Communication difficulties often occur when a client's expectations do not align with the circumstances. How can you prevent these kinds of communication problems?

It is plausible that your client lacks a firm grasp of the industry or depends on false presumptions or facts. They may think their current house should sell for far more than its true and fair market value, or they could think they should be able to buy a new one at an unreasonably low price.

The following are some strategies you can use to moderate your client's expectations while keeping lines of communication open:

1. It's typical for buyers and sellers to have irrational expectations when they first enter the market; find out what they anticipate. They may also have misconceptions about what you do as a realtor, how much they are willing to pay, or how long it should take them to buy or sell a property. The expectations of certain customers may be influenced by watching

reality television programmes about house renovations and property flipping.

You'd be surprised at how many misunderstandings you can prevent by asking your client up front what their expectations are. You can prevent problems from getting out of control by determining what your clients anticipate from you.

Refraining from "correcting" them could come out as patronizing. Just let them know how the market is doing right now. When they discover that their expectations aren't even close to being fulfilled, they may feel a little down, but that's preferable to the potential anger and discontent that may develop later on if their unrealistic expectations are maintained for an extended period.

You can directly address these issues by posing questions during your initial meeting. Take your clients step-by-step through the entire procedure and address any queries they may have.

2. Tell Them About the Internet: The Internet is arguably the best communication tool ever created. We now have easy access to information at our fingers. On the other hand, the problem of misleading information is getting more and more obvious. There is a lot of inaccurate and misleading information on real estate online.

False information may be a nightmare for a real estate agent whose clients look up information online about buying or selling a property. Some clients might take what they read as true, whether outdated or just plain false. Of course, you can't stop children from using the computer, but you can tell them that a lot of the material they get online isn't reliable and could even be more dangerous than helpful. Tell them to come see you first if they have any questions, allowing them to "verify" the information you provide online if they so choose.

3. Develop Mutual Trust: You and your client must have much mutual trust for a client-realtor relationship. Many of your customers will make one of their largest purchases with this buy. Some may have to give up their home for an extended period. It makes sense that they might be a little anxious and apprehensive. Sometimes, you have to tell your clients that you have their best interests in mind. You should stay in regular contact with them even if there isn't any news to report. Find out a little about their interests, family, and life events outside of real estate. When the time comes, instead of getting a second opinion from an agent who might mislead or overpromise, they will pay attention to your advice and trust it. Relationships are strengthened when people stay in touch. Developing a solid rapport with your clients has to be your first concern.

4. Refrain from Overselling: Have you heard the saying "Under promise and over deliver"? It functions flawlessly while working with real estate clients.

When big sums of money and exquisite residences are involved, it can be simple for individuals to become enthused; when you can't, don't suggest. Don't mislead others into thinking this is a "great time to buy."

The bottom line is always being honest with your clients, even when neither of you wants to hear it. If you keep things grounded, your clients will find things a lot easier and have greater faith in you.

5. Since you work as a real estate agent in this field daily, understand their situation. You know the trade's tricks, techniques, ins and outs. However, your clients are likely unaware of the true situation.

You can seem like their only hope as a realtor because many people find the real estate industry daunting. Investigate the possible causes of their fear, desire to make a poor decision, or lack of confidence. Where does the fear come from? If you can relate to their situation and understand what they are going through, you can give them the greatest advice in a way that they will listen to.

Assure your clients that you are sensitive to their needs and will work through challenging moments with them. Inform them that you will be available to answer any questions and that they should not hesitate. Empathy is one of the most important traits of a salesperson or real estate agent.

Taking Care of Your Customers: The consumer might not always be right, at least not in the details. While their needs, wants, and aspirations are undoubtedly the most important, it is your job as a professional to control their expectations and inform them about the real estate market. Being open, honest, genuine, helpful, and knowledgeable will give you the best chance of controlling their expectations and assisting them in reaching their ultimate goals.

In the current real estate market, clients need individualized attention from their brokers. If you are unaware of the newest trends and technologies, you will be wasting your and your customers' time. When you're ready to take charge of your future, use these pointers to offer your company the required advantage.

- Be accessible,
- Establish objectives,

Make a marketing strategy,

Develop as an Authority in Your Field

- Establish Connections
- Boost Your Involvement on Social Media

Put Small Business Systems Into Practice

Don't Just Pay Attention to Selling 1. Be Available: You will lose money and potential clients if you can't offer each client your attention, even if you're working with five at once.

● With Caller ID, answering the phone and learning more about possible clients is simpler than ever. Of course, there will be occasions when you cannot get on the phone promptly; nonetheless, take a call from a current client if you can. It is most likely a simple problem with a simple fix for them. You will be hero material if you lend them a helping hand for even five minutes. When you weigh the alternatives, you may be shocked to learn how crucial availability is to the average small business.

Finding out each client's preferred mode of contact is equally crucial. Which do they prefer: texting, emails, or regular phone calls?

Make sure you communicate with them on that platform, no matter how they answer. Your clients will notice when you make the effort to tailor their experience and pay attention to the "small things."

~ Establish Goals: Did you realize that 83% of people don't have any? Furthermore, only 3% of individuals who make goals put them in writing. But if you put your goals down in writing, your chances of success will increase by 79 per cent. With such a figure, there's no excuse not to incorporate goal-setting into your everyday business operations.

Setting goals is essential for all real estate entrepreneurs who wish to thrive because they provide a means of monitoring and evaluating their progress. How can you tell whether your business is improving if you don't know how you compare to the competitors? Setting clear, quantifiable, executable, reasonable, and time-bound goals is a guaranteed method to ensure success.

~ Establish a Marketing Strategy You will have a significant advantage if you can automate creating a marketing campaign. Success with automated marketing requires three things:

you have to cover all the bases and customize every consumer interaction without starting from scratch with a fresh campaign. Use both conventional and contemporary marketing techniques to attract a wide audience, and make sure you know who your target clients are. Once you have found an approach that works for you, you may duplicate the process across multiple mediums. You can find that the information on your direct mail piece flows into a social media post and vice versa. Never stop searching for methods to improve productivity; don't be afraid to use your imagination.

Become an expert in your field by learning everything you can about it. Because information about anything and everything can be accessible online, homebuyers are less inclined to engage the services of real estate brokers and investors. Read the blogs on Redfin or Trulia and find all the answers for free. Ultimately, the only thing an agent can offer clients that the internet can't match is experience. If you position yourself as a thought leader or an authority in your profession, prospective homebuyers will be compelled to cooperate with you.

Kris Lippi, the licenced real estate broker behind ISoldMyHouse.com, advises staying in your neighbourhood because a solid reputation is crucial. Your chances of gaining business will increase because, as he says, "the real estate industry heavily relies on referrals." Practising where people know you naturally provides you with credibility.

Keeping up with industry news and concentrating on your local market are the greatest ways to succeed.

~ Make connections: The schedule of a good real estate agent is never empty. That does not, however, imply that you should forgo cultivating client relationships. Always going above and beyond is required in every transaction. Long nights and late hours should not be the exception, at least not for a while. It has never been stated that achieving greater success will be easy. It shouldn't matter if you sell a house for $200,000 or $20 million; you should treat every customer equally.

Juggling Education with Other Objectives

It's critical to balance saving for school and other financial objectives. Considering objectives like homeownership, retirement, and other family requirements, consider how saving for college fits your overall financial plan.

Promoting Accountability

Include your kids in discussions regarding their schooling as they get older. Instruct children on money's worth and stress the need to save and create a budget. Urge them to use scholarships or part-time employment to help pay for their education.

Making educational plans for your kids shows your dedication as a parent and an investment in their future success. It's about giving them the resources to realize their aspirations, not just paying for their books and tuition.

Making Retirement Plans Together

Retirement planning is a shared vision for your future as a partnership, not merely a financial objective. Even though it could seem far off when you're just starting a life together, retirement is a goal that needs to be prioritised from the beginning of your financial journey. Why is it so crucial for a couple to plan for retirement?

A Single, Shared Vision

Planning for retirement compels you and your spouse to have similar future goals. It starts a dialogue about your hopes, dreams, and plans for the years after you take a break from the grind. These talks are crucial to creating a solid, cohesive front in your marriage.

Calculating Retirement Requirements

Calculating how much you'll need to sustain your ideal lifestyle in retirement is the first step in retirement planning. This entails considering your existing way of life, anticipated spending, and the age at which you both hope to retire. To ensure you're well-prepared, estimating with realism and thoroughness is critical.

Employer Retirement Plans: Utilise Them

Retirement plans with great benefits, like 401(k)s, are provided by many workplaces. Couples must seize these chances to the fullest. To optimise matching contributions, ensure you contribute a sufficient amount to your employer-sponsored retirement plans. This improves your overall financial security in addition to increasing your retirement funds.

Investing Portfolio Diversification

Planning for retirement entails making prudent investments to support your funds' long-term growth. Work with a financial advisor to build a diversified investment strategy that fits your risk tolerance and retirement objectives. By distributing risk, diversification raises the possibility that you will meet your long-term financial goals.

Periodic Evaluation and Modifications

A static document should not be your retirement plan. Personal objectives, financial markets, and life situations all fluctuate over time. You and your partner must examine and tweak your retirement plan regularly. By taking the initiative, you can ensure you stay on course to reach your retirement objectives.

The Strength of Combining

Your retirement funds may be greatly impacted by starting early. Over time, compound interest may be quite beneficial, and the earlier you start saving, the more time your investments have to appreciate. Adopt a consistent savings strategy as a pair, and see your nest egg grow over time.

Getting Ready for a Rewarding Retirement

Retirement offers the chance to live a happy and meaningful life, not just financial security. Together, decide how you want to spend your retirement years: talking about hobbies, trips, volunteer work, or anything else that makes you two happy.

One of the most important aspects of your financial journey as a marriage is retirement planning. Creating a shared vision for your golden years and taking proactive measures to turn that vision into reality is more important than worrying about money. You can start your retirement journey with joy and confidence, knowing your collaboration will make your retirement years truly golden. Your partnership can work together to estimate your needs, leverage workplace programmes, diversify your investments, and routinely monitor your progress.

S Corporation Restraints: Possible Consequences

Even though S corporations have a lot of advantages, it's important to consider any potential disadvantages before forming one. Knowing these boundaries will enable you to make a choice consistent with your entrepreneurial journey. Let's examine the other viewpoint and clarify any possible difficulties you might have.

Qualifiability Standards

Unlike several other forms of corporate formations, a S Corporation has specific qualifications to be eligible. For instance, there's a ceiling on the number of shareholders, usually set at 100, and all of them must be citizens or permanent residents of the United States. These conditions can make bringing in foreign investors or increasing ownership more difficult.

Forms and the Weight of Administration

Selecting a S Corporation requires you to assume more managerial duties. It will be necessary for you to keep correct records, follow certain procedures, and schedule frequent shareholder meetings. These standards can result in more time and administrative demands, even if they are crucial for upholding the company's credibility.

Restricted Adjustment in Profit Distribution

A proportionate payout based on each shareholder's ownership percentage is required for an S Corporation instead of a partnership or LLC, which frequently permits flexible profit allocation. Due to this restriction, You might be unable to adjust profit sharing among shareholders.

Limitations on Shareholder Types

Certain entities, such as partnerships or other corporations, are not permitted to be stockholders of S corporations. This restriction can make it more difficult to set up investment agreements or include specific kinds of investors.

Possible Loss Restrictions

There can be restrictions on how much loss a shareholder in an S Corporation can write off on their tax returns. This limitation may affect the ability to deduct company losses from other sources of income.

It's crucial to remember that a S Corporation has advantages that these restrictions should not outweigh. Instead, they are things to consider and assess in light of your business requirements and objectives. You may proactively address possible issues and create plans to lessen their influence on your company by being aware of them.

Recall that considering all relevant aspects, such as your long-term goals, expansion strategies, and financial targets, is essential to making an informed choice on your company structure. Consulting with legal and tax experts can offer priceless insights and enable you to handle these issues confidently.

We'll thoroughly compare S Corporations and other company entities in the following section. You'll be able to decide if an S Corporation is the best option for your entrepreneurial path by knowing how it compares to the competition. Let's compare the two and keep looking for the ideal business entity match.

S Corporations and Other Business Entities: A Comparative Analysis

It is important to consider how an S Corporation differs from other structures accessible to entrepreneurs such as yourself when you find yourself at the crossroads of business entity alternatives. Understanding the differences and similarities might help you decide on a plan of action that meets your goals and preferences. Now, let's get into a thorough comparison that will highlight the special characteristics of a S Corporation.

Partnership and Sole Proprietorship

Unlike partnerships and sole proprietorships, S Corporations offer limited liability protection and segregate personal and corporate assets. This protection can be a big benefit compared to general partnerships and sole proprietorships, where personal assets are vulnerable.

C Company

The tax treatment of a S Corporation is not the same as that of a C Corporation. A C Corporation is subject to double taxes on its corporate income and shareholder dividends, whereas an S Corporation benefits from pass-through taxation. A S Corporation has limitations on the quantity and kind of shareholders, whereas a C Corporation allows multiple classes of stock and an unlimited number of owners.

Companies with limited liability have both limited liability protection and pass-through taxation. There are noticeable distinctions, though. Compared to S Corporations, LLCs have fewer formal restrictions and administrative burdens, as well as greater. An S Corporation, however, might provide more authority and distinction.

When choosing between an S Corporation and other business organisations, it's important to consider liability protection, tax ramifications, ownership and management flexibility, administrative requirements, and long-term growth objectives. Making the best decision for your organisation will be guided by considering your unique needs, objectives, and vision.

Please be aware that this choice is subject to change. You might discover that switching between entities is advantageous or required as your firm develops. Speaking with legal and tax experts who can evaluate your situation and offer customised guidance to help you make decisions is crucial.

We'll focus on the important query: Is an S Corporation the best option for you? in the following section. You can determine whether this business entity fits your entrepreneurial goals by reviewing some important factors. Now, let's proceed and examine the elements that will direct you towards making a wise choice.

☐ Useful guidance and resources for creating and overseeing many sources of income

The following resources and helpful tips can help you establish and run your alternative revenue stream:

Investing: Begin by familiarising yourself with the various investing possibilities and associated dangers. The Motley Fool, Seeking

Alpha, and Investopedia. Sites like Charles Schwab, E*TRADE, and Robinhood. Be ready to periodically review your investments and modify your action plan as necessary.

When starting a freelance career, determine what services and abilities you can provide to possible clients. Make a website to highlight your services and a portfolio of your work. Utilise online marketplaces such as Fiverr, Freelancer, or Upwork to locate possible assignments and clients. Prepare yourself to handle your time and task and bargain for better prices.

Entrepreneurship: To begin, decide what kind of goods or services you want and conduct market research to substantiate your concept. Make a business plan and, if required, obtain funding. Consider selling your goods or services online using sites like Shopify or Etsy. Be ready to oversee your own time, money, and advertising campaigns.

Finding a passive income source that fits your hobbies and abilities should be your first step in generating passive money. Think about investing in dividend-paying equities or buying rental properties...

Managing your alternative income sources with diligence and discipline is crucial, so be ready to constantly research and check on your investments. It's important to keep track of your earnings and outlays, budget for taxes, and always seek methods to expand and enhance your sources of revenue. Additionally, many online networks and tools are available, such as Facebook groups and Reddit forums, where you may interact with others pursuing comparable revenue streams and gain knowledge from their experiences.

Developing and marketing virtual education

Share your knowledge with others and get passive income. Choose a subject that you are educated about, and that has a market that is prepared to pay for it first. Do market research to verify your concept and determine whether there is a market for your course. Next, create a thorough course outline covering all themes, lessons, learning objectives, and assessments. When creating the content and structure of your course, choose a platform such as Thinkific or Teachable. Next, combine written, audio, and video content to produce interesting and dynamic course materials. Invest in high-quality hardware and software to guarantee your course has a polished appearance and sound.

Promote your course to prospective students by using. A free trial or discount could be provided to pique curiosity and encourage membership.

Launch your course: To create buzz and increase sales, decide on a launch date and develop a marketing strategy. Use websites such as Coursera, Skillshare, and Udemy to host and sell your course.

Track your course metrics, including enrollment, completion rates, and student feedback, to monitor your outcomes. Use this information to change and modify your marketing plans and course content.

books published independently on Amazon KDP

One well-liked method for making passive money and receiving royalties is self-publishing novels on Amazon KDP. Here are some useful hints and resources to get you going:

Select a topic that interests you, has a market for it, and that people are prepared to pay for. Do some market research to verify your concept and determine whether there is a market for your book.

Write your book: Use a word processor such as Google Docs or Microsoft Word to write and format your book. To ensure your book is flawless and error-free, think about using an editor or proofreader.

Publish your book: Make sure it appears in relevant searches by selecting the right categories and keywords when uploading and publishing it using Amazon's KDP programme.

Promote your book: Consider providing a complimentary preview or discount to spark curiosity and encourage purchases.

Keep an eye on your outcomes: Keep tabs on the sales and reviews of your book. Utilise this data to tweak and enhance your content and marketing efforts.

Producing and marketing digital goods via the internet

One excellent method to create additional revenue streams is through the creation and online sale of digital goods. Here are some useful hints and resources to get you going:

Select your product: Decide on a product you are informed about and believe there is a market for. eBooks, courses, software, graphics, templates, and audio/video files are a few examples of digital products.

Make your product: To design and build your product, use a digital creation tool such as Canva, Adobe Creative Suite, or Figma. Think about collaborating with someone who can produce a high-quality product or hiring a freelancer.

Create your online store: To create and sell your things online, use an e-commerce platform such as Shopify, Gumroad, or WooCommerce. Make sure the look and feel of your store reflect your brand and draw in customers.

Market your product: To reach potential buyers, advertise your product online via social media, email marketing, and other channels. A free sample or demo might be provided to spark interest and encourage purchases.

Deliver your product: After a consumer makes a purchase, use an online delivery company like SendOwl or E-junkie to safely deliver your product to them. Streamline your productivity and save time by automating the delivery process.

Keep an eye on your results: Keep tabs on the sales and reviews of your product. Utilise this data to tweak and enhance your content and marketing efforts.

Investment in real estate

is a method to create wealth and income over time. Here are some useful hints and resources to get you going:

Investigate the market: Learn as much as possible about the local or prospective investment area's real estate markets. Consider elements such as local laws, rent demand, and property valuations.

Create a plan: Choose your investment approach, such as real estate investment trusts

(REITs), purchasing and keeping rents, or flipping properties. Create a strategy for financing your assets and overseeing your real estate.

Find possible homes: Use internet listing services like Redfin or Zillow to find properties that fit your investment criteria. Think of things like potential for appreciation, condition, and location.

Examine the property: Perform a comprehensive examination of the property, encompassing a market analysis, a financial analysis, and a property inspection. Ascertain the possible dangers and challenges and the potential return on investment (ROI).

Finance the investment: Select a financing solution per your financial objectives and investment strategy. Hard money loans, private funding, and conventional mortgages are possible options.

Handle the property: If you intend to keep rental properties, you might want to think about using a property management business to take care of daily tasks. By doing this, you can guarantee that your properties are well-maintained and save time.

Track your investments, pay attention to your cash flow and ROI, and monitor your results. Make adjustments to optimise your returns and reach your financial objectives as necessary.

You may learn more about real estate investing via various online forums and tools, such as the Real Estate Investor Summit podcast and the BiggerPockets website and podcast. By participating in online seminars, you can gain insightful knowledge about current trends and practical advice to help you succeed in real estate investing.

Kim's Corner: The Secret Is Acceptance!

Everybody experiences puberty at a different time, which results in varying rates of physical change. This implies that the effects of hormones on you and your peers differ. I assure you that everyone worries, at least somewhat, about what other people think. Try to keep yourself in mind and embrace where you are right now. In this brief stage of life, everything will change and not remain the same for very long.

If you have bad thoughts about THEIR hygiene practices, please hold off on saying anything to someone.

Please let it be if you see someone in class with an odd smell, foul breath, or unclean nails. Making a point out of this is completely unnecessary, especially in public. Believe me. They are in the process of coming to terms with who they are. It might be harmful to bring this up humiliatingly for that person.

Please be considerate. All of us are human. Each person has a unique path with various cultural and ethnic backgrounds. Simply accept them for who they are. Let them worry about themselves while you worry about yourself.

If you feel comfortable speaking with this friend, there's always a way to be friendly. After lunch, for instance, you might wish to inform your friend that they have something stuck in their teeth. However, be tactful and speak discreetly to avoid embarrassing them in front of others. Make sense?

QUARTER

wholesome behaviours

W

What exactly is a habit? A *habit* is a habitual, subconsciously performed behaviour that is repeated regularly.

You've likely adopted various habits—some positive, some not so good—from parents, friends, the media, and other sources. I'll concentrate on the best ways to take care of your physical health, including what you eat, how active you are, and how well you sleep.

Let's Discuss Nutrition!

Your body receives all the nutrients it needs to function at its best when it is fed properly. You feel good, your body functions properly, and you eat well. Easy enough?

I know you've heard this before, but let me reiterate. You have to take care of your body!

Advantages of Healthy Eating

Here's why paying attention to what you eat only makes sense.

Control of Weight

Making the appropriate meal selections will probably help you maintain a healthier weight. Physical changes during adolescence include growth spurts, which may cause you to become more ravenous. You can eat more while maintaining a healthy weight by making healthful choices.

Lowers Disease Risk

Illnesses exist, people! Furthermore, they don't only affect the elderly. A healthy diet makes your body happy and robust, enabling you to be at your best when fending against illness.

strengthens the immune system

I know pretending to be ill and occasionally skipping school might be enjoyable. However, when you're seriously unwell, things change. Nobody enjoys feeling ill and frail. When you eat well, your body is powerful and can fend off illness much more successfully.

Enhanced Vitality

Maintaining your energy levels with good food and exercise—which we'll discuss briefly—allows you to enjoy all your activities.

Delays the Ageing Process

Acquire this! Do you want to look like an 18-year-old instead of 38? Maintaining your youthful appearance starts with eating a healthy diet.

Improved Skin (few pimples)

I understand that the enormous zit that appeared out of nowhere just before the first day of class feels like the worst thing that could happen to you. Oh no... You will have healthier, brighter Skin if you follow a balanced diet.

Aids in Concentration

Sugar-filled foods and beverages lack healthy calories and nutrients. Even while you need calories for energy, it's much worse for you when they don't provide any nutritious benefit. Instead, fuel your body and mind with wholesome nutrients.

Encourages Mental Well-Being

You feel right when you eat right. Nutritious meals support a clean body. And doing this keeps your thoughts clear.

You require additional nutrition as a teenager to support the development of your bones, hormones, and other bodily systems, including your brain. Try to avoid eating out, sugar-filled beverages, and highly processed foods. Additionally, don't forget to choose healthy meals and snacks, drink water, and eat breakfast.

A. Various Investment Choices and Their Benefits and Drawbacks

Various investing choices exist, each having pros and cons of their own. We'll look at popular investment choices:

Equities Stocks are a company's ownership shares. Long-term growth and the possibility of large returns are two benefits of stocks. But stocks can also be volatile and come with a lot of risk.

Bonds: Bonds are government or corporate loans. Bonds have set and consistent returns as one of their benefits. Bonds, however, are also susceptible to inflation and interest rates.

Real estate benefits from steady income flows and possible large returns. Real estate, however, may be expensive and needs upkeep.

Mutual funds are investment portfolios that are professionally managed. Professional portfolio management and simple diversification are two benefits of mutual funds. But administration costs might add up.

B. How to Assess the Risks of Investing and Make Well-Informed Decisions

There is always some risk involved with investing. We will look at the many hazards connected to each investment option and how to assess risks according to your investment profile. We will also review how to assess investment success using metrics like the risk/return ratio.

Risks Associated with Stocks: Market risk, volatility, and liquidity are risks connected to stocks. Understanding the industry and the firm you are investing in is crucial for assessing the risks involved with stock transactions.

Bond-Related Risks: Interest rate risk, inflation risk, and credit risk are some of the risks connected to bonds. Knowing the issuer's credit rating and the current interest rate is crucial for assessing the risks involved in bond investing.

Risks Associated with Real Estate: Investing in real estate carries certain risks, such as market, rental, and maintenance. It's critical to comprehend the local real estate market to assess the risks of real estate investing.

To sum up, financial freedom requires understanding how to invest and accept measured risks. Furthermore, you may optimise profits while reducing potential losses by assessing the risks involved in each investment and making well-informed selections. You can also get better results by avoiding common blunders like emotional decision-making and a lack of diversification. In the end, investing is an ongoing process. Therefore, you should be ready to adjust your strategy and learn from changing market conditions.

Communication is a two-way process. An excellent communicator must comprehend what others are attempting to communicate.

Knowing what others say about a subject makes it easier to investigate opposing viewpoints before developing your own. Furthermore, listening skillfully will promote trust and understanding between people.

To have excellent communication, you need to be an attentive listener. Possessing empathy and patience are also beneficial. They understand that they must listen without talking.

An effective communication style is essential for academic success.

During communication, information is exchanged both orally and nonverbally.

Information communication skills are more crucial than actual knowledge. By doing this, you can reach the fullest extent of your potential.

Communication skills improve your vocabulary and cognitive growth.

This aids in completing writing homework for school. It also helps you do well in school presentations, essential for enhancing your confidence.

Boost your sense of value and self-worth.

Because they can set boundaries, communicate with others, and feel confident in their identity, teenagers with great communication skills also tend to have higher self-esteem.

Boost your originality.

Effective communicators in their teens can also express themselves creatively in different contexts. It might help you discover your creative side and develop your self-worth.

Expand your creativity.

Teens who express their thoughts and feelings through language can expand and free their imaginations. We require the right language and communication skills to tell stories, make games, and try out different play techniques. These are critical skills for development.

Promote creative thinking.

Teens who can communicate effectively can better voice their thoughts and encourage candid dialogue, enhancing their capacity to think for themselves.

Speaking with others benefits you. It gives you confidence boosts and encourages you to establish your own opinions.

Enhance your problem-solving skills.

Communication is the key to problem-solving. Teens with good communication skills seek solutions and try different team-building strategies.

Make strong ties and contacts.

By speaking with individuals, you will establish and maintain bonds and relationships with them.

Teens must communicate well if they are to feel supported and self-assured, as well as establish strong bonds with their teachers and peers.

How to Improve Your Teenage Communication Skills

You want to prepare as much as you can as a teenager for maturity, college, the workforce, and high school.

Developing your communication abilities is one of the keys to your success in the future.

How to Improve Your Teenage Communication Skills

Speak less and pay closer attention.

One way to improve communication skills is to listen carefully to the other person before formulating your response, as people like to feel heard.

The person speaking to you should be your life's most important person.

Seek clarity and have one conversation at a time to avoid misunderstandings.

This suggests that you should refrain from replying to emails or texts when speaking with someone on the phone and from listening intently before doing so.

2. Recognise who your audience is.

Your speech will vary depending on who you are speaking to.

Using informal language like "Hey" and "TTYL" is acceptable when chatting with a friend. You should refrain from doing so if you are speaking with or messaging your manager, tutor, instructor, or supervisor.

You can't assume that someone else understands the colloquial language you use with your friends. If you want to improve your communication abilities, remember the other person when you are communicating.

3. Body language is crucial.

Effective communication is essential in both face-to-face and virtual meetings.

Maintaining an open stance suggests that you are personable. Keep your arms extended and make eye contact with the other person to demonstrate that you are paying attention to them.

Try to look at the camera instead of the screen in a video conference. It changes things drastically.

4. Before sending your emails, proofread them.

Checking your grammar and spelling is important. Check your writing one more time to ensure the words you use to communicate convey the intended meaning.

Keep it brief but specific enough to get your point across. After composing your message, put it away and come back to it at a later time.

Before hitting the submit button, think about how you would reply if this were emailed. If you are responding to an email, read it through to the end before writing anything.

5. Write down your ideas.

If you want to improve your communication abilities, take exact notes like in a lecture.

Recalling things at a meeting or conversing with someone else is not a good idea.

Send a follow-up email to ensure you understand what was said during the conversation.

Without coming across as awkward, you may mention to the individual you're conversing with that taking notes is a practice that helps you stay organised. This is quite helpful for networking.

6. Sometimes it's better to pick up the phone.

When you find that you have a lot to say, give someone a call instead of sending a message. Direct messages on social media or emails work great for certain types of communication. However, since a two-way conversation permits natural ebbs and flows, there are occasions when it is preferable.

7. Talk slowly while you speak.

Always pause for a breath before speaking, and show consideration for everyone you encounter. Think carefully about the words you want to use, and pay attention to how you pronounce them.

If you can get yourself to think things through before you speak, the audience will perceive you as more mature and responsible.

8. Have a positive attitude and a grin.

Your grin and upbeat demeanour will make people feel good about you. This still holds when you're on the phone; your speech will sound different if you smile and focus on a cheerful attitude.

This straightforward habit is sometimes overlooked yet has a big impact on many of your lectures.

Increasing Your Earnings

A. Assessing Present Revenue Sources

Reaching your objectives and becoming financially successful requires increasing your revenue. It's important to begin by assessing your current sources of revenue to grow your profits successfully. This chapter will walk you through evaluating your current income, looking into other options, bargaining for a better wage and benefits, and growing your career.

1. Evaluating Your Present Salary

Start by assessing the sources of income you currently have, such as wages, salary, or revenue from self-employment. Consider any extra perks you may receive, including commissions, bonuses, or profit-sharing. Knowing your current sources of income will help you pinpoint areas for growth and establish reasonable objectives for raising your revenue.

2. Examining Your Work Performance: Evaluate your performance and pinpoint areas where you may improve. Examine your contributions, achievements, and strong points. If you want a more complete picture of your strengths and areas for improvement, think about asking for feedback from colleagues or superiors. Assessing how well you do at work might help you find ways to provide value and even earn more money.

3. Finding Skill Deficits

Determine the skills you lack and how much you could make. Examine the credentials and abilities in demand in your sector or area of specialization. Take chances for professional growth, such as workshops, certificates, or further education, to gain the skills you need and improve your marketability.

B. Examining Different Sources of Income

While making the most of your current income is crucial, looking into new revenue streams can greatly increase your total earnings. We'll cover a variety of strategies for increasing the diversity of your income and generating new sources of income in this section.

1. Freelancing and Side Businesses

Use your interests or abilities to leverage freelancing. This could entail tuition, graphic design, freelance writing, and consulting services. There are many chances in the gig economy to make money from your skills and generate extra revenue.

2. Streams of Passive Income

You can use passive revenue streams with little to no continuous work. Some examples are peer-to-peer financing, dividend-paying stocks, real estate rental income, and the development and marketing of digital goods. While it takes work and upfront commitment to develop passive income, it can eventually yield a consistent revenue stream.

3. Making Money Using Your Assets

Determine which goods or assets you can sell. For instance, you might consider renting extra space on websites like Airbnb. Consider alternatives like ride-sharing or food delivery services if you own a car. You are monetizing more money by monetizing your assets by making the most of your current assets.

4. Online Business or E-commerce: Launching an online company or e-commerce endeavour can be a successful means of making money. Whether you design and promote goods, give coaching or advisory services, or open an online store, the Internet offers a worldwide market with many growth prospects.

C. Haggling about Pay and Benefits

Negotiating your salary and perks is a good strategy to boost your income and enhance your total pay package. You can obtain better financial terms by standing up for yourself and proving your worth. When negotiating pay and benefits, keep the following in mind: 1. Examine Market Prices.

Find out the pay scales and industry norms for your position and experience level. Industry publications and internet resources might offer insightful information. Equipped with this knowledge, you can confidently discuss pay expectations during negotiations.

2. EEmphasizeYour Worth

Make sure you express your value to the company in the negotiations. Talk about your accomplishments, contributions, and the good you have done. Give concrete instances of how you have outperformed expectations and contributed to the organization.

3. Stress Your Knowledge and Experience

Emphasize your distinctive abilities, knowledge, and any specialized education or qualifications you may hold. Proving that you have unique or in-demand abilities will help you negotiate and support a larger salary.

4. Be Willing to Make Sacrifices

are the goals of negotiations. If a pay raise is not immediately possible, be willing to make concessions and look into other types of compensation, such as bonuses, performance-based incentives, or more vacation time.

5. Engage in Effective Communication

During negotiations, effective communication is essential. In your conversations, project assurance, assertiveness, and professionalism. Actively hear the other side out and give a considered response. Before the discussion, practice your negotiating techniques to feel more at ease and ready.

D. Developing Your Career for Greater Earnings

Professional development is a long-term approach to raising your earning potential. You may set yourself up for more possibilities and higher income by constantly developing your knowledge, seeking professional progression options, and upgrading your abilities. Take into account the following tactics for career advancement:

1. Ongoing Education

industry developments, attending seminars or conferences and obtaining pertinent degrees or certifications. Seize the chance to further your career by expanding your knowledge and skill set, increasing your employability.

2. Look for More Accountabilities

Show that you are ambitious and open to more duties in your existing position. Offer to coach new coworkers, provide creative ideas, or volunteer for difficult jobs. You can raise your chances of getting a raise in pay or promotion by demonstrating your dependability and proactive attitude.

3. Create Connections and Networking

Professional development requires networking. Join associations for professionals, go to industry events, and make connections with mentors and coworkers in your area. Developing a robust professional network provides access to new

prospects, such as partnerships, employment recommendations, and future career progression.

4. Go for Higher Education

To improve your marketability and knowledge, consider obtaining higher education, such as a master's degree or specialized certificates. Look into programs that give chances for professional development and correspond with your career objectives. 5. Seek Professionals and Mentors

Section Six

Establishing and fulfilling goals

The word "goals" is thrown around in society these days with great casualness. to the point where it's simple to forget what a goal is.

What sets goals apart from other kinds of objectives and resolutions?

Why is setting objectives necessary?

The process of defining and achieving goals is clearly related, according to a study from the psychologist and career counsellor at the Dominican University of California. Inadequately worded goals can hinder the formation of new habits and divert your attention from your priorities.

Setting certain goals is not the only thing involved. Additionally, completing them is important.

Together, we will examine some of the best approaches for setting and achieving personal and professional goals.

What precisely are objectives, and what are they not?

To set goals for oneself, you must first grasp what a goal entails.

A goal can be defined as "something you wish to get done." It is the ultimate objective you or a group of people deliberately set out to achieve.

Goals are typically oriented toward the far future. This includes long-term goals for businesses or organizations and plans for people's lives and professions.

Alternatively expressed, a goal is a dream with a deadline.

Are you a little perplexed now? Here are a few characteristics of objectives and some things they are not.

One goal is:

Your future-focused perspective. Your goals should be heavily influenced by your vision statement and the objectives you have established for yourself.

Temporary in nature. The most fruitful goals are those that have time constraints. The time horizon for goals is typically far longer. Subsequently, smaller, more achievable objectives could be deduced from the bigger ones.

Vast in character. Aim for something that initially seems unattainable without fear. You can think beyond the box and set high standards for yourself. Perhaps the best way to get there is to finish off some of your easier, shorter-term goals first.

A goal differs from the following:

An objective. While objectives are the tasks that must be done to achieve goals, goals are declarations of what you hope to achieve. Since this is the objective, an example of a goal may be, "I want to become a confident public speaker." The goal is to work with a coach to improve your public speaking abilities by the end of this month.

A decision. Most resolutions only intend to last temporarily and bring about immediate fulfilment (as opposed to delayed pleasure). A resolution is a decision on whether or not to take on a task.

An undertaking. A clear and narrow path is formed due to the formulation of mission statements. The mission statement is the cornerstone that guides the operations of a company, organization or individual. Conversely, a goal is a specific target that you and your team work to accomplish.

Why should your group set goals for itself, and why should you?

A summary of the many reasons why goal-setting is crucial for both individuals and teams can be seen below.

It provides a precise outline of the next steps.

One might acquire a sense of purpose and direction by periodically reflecting on their goals.

For example, you may develop a plan for the coming years based on your idealized image of your life over those five years. This long-term plan could help you transition from the stage of simply dreaming to the one of actually doing.

Setting goals for your team at work aids in determining the course that the group will follow going forward. Setting expectations for the different team members is also beneficial.

One advantage of making goals for ourselves is that it allows us to stand back and see what's important in life. It's the first step to creating a fulfilling life for yourself.

Setting goals together as a group at work helps everyone get a better knowledge of the bigger picture. If all team members know the organization's long-term objectives and what the company is striving toward, they may perform better in their given roles.

It is a wellspring of creativity.

When you set goals for yourself consciously, you have something to strive toward by default. You and your team will be more driven to give your best effort if you have a specific goal.

Understanding the objectives of the team you are working with can inspire and motivate you as a member. Your team will have a sense of purpose if you can motivate and reward yourself while helping the group move closer to a common goal.

It gives you greater control over how your destiny unfolds.

The first step towards taking charge of your life is to set goals. The act of writing down your goals signifies that you are actively identifying what it is that you want out of life.

It's the first action you should do to begin controlling your destiny.

Section Three

Advice on how to save without sacrificing your needs

Savings on regular spending

One excellent method to manage your money well without compromising your quality of life is to save money on regular expenses. There are no secret ways to save an additional €100 every month. You can, however, heed a few pieces of advice.

The following advice will help you reduce your daily expenses:

Make a weekly meal plan to help you make the most of your food purchases and prevent waste. In bulk, customize your menu to fit current promotions.

Before heading out to the store, compile a list of the things you must have. Impulsive purchases can quickly add up in expenses. Another well-known yet helpful hint is to avoid shopping when you're hungry. You will inevitably purchase more items or items in less sensible amounts. Thus, before you go shopping, ensure you've eaten or are not hungry.

Examine prices: Before purchasing, compare costs at several retailers or online. You can locate the greatest offers and save money in this way. Some brands cost more than others, particularly in large cities.

Use public transportation or carpooling: If possible, reduce your trip expenses. You will contribute to environmental preservation in addition to saving money. Once, when I turned onto the road to work, I noticed that one of my coworkers was travelling the same route. I asked him for directions when I got there and discovered that not only was I his neighbour, but I was also travelling the same path. We so decided to travel and return together. We both saved money by doing this, and our cars also saw reduced wear and tear.

Lower energy expenses: Make environmentally conscious decisions to reduce energy use, such as insulating your home, using low-energy lightbulbs, and turning off electrical appliances when not in use. With these actions, you'll save money on energy expenses, particularly on heating bills.

Free or inexpensive services: Research free or inexpensive events happening in your city for entertainment and cultural pursuits. You'll be able to have fun without going over budget. For instance, the first Sunday of each month is free admission to museums in a few French cities. This is an excellent method to travel without breaking the bank.

Take up certain tasks alone: You can cut down on some daily costs by taking up some tasks alone. For instance, you can perform minor repairs and maintenance independently or cook at home rather than getting takeout. Most of the time, things are easier than they seem. And perhaps you'd prefer to. I firmly believe that many people love to cook but aren't aware of it since they place orders frequently or love do-it-yourself projects but make purchases too rapidly.

Modify your diet: Some items are pricey, so be cautious when you get life-altering news. For instance, meat can be very pricey sometimes, but it can be readily substituted with less expensive meats like poultry or veggie protein sources like tofu. Furthermore, frozen veggies are frequently affordable. I'm not advocating giving up meat entirely; I'm just saying cut back. The same is true for alcohol and sugary drinks: water is always more affordable and healthier than a bottle of booze or sugar.

Quality of life by using these strategies. Keep in mind that every little bit helps, and when these savings mount up, they can make a big difference in your budget and assist you in reaching your financial objectives.

Benefit from sales and exclusive deals.

Using sales and discounts is a wise method to cut costs without compromising quality of life. Keeping a healthy budget requires the skill of grasping opportunities when they arise. Here are some pointers for maximizing beneficial deals.

First and foremost, knowledge is power. Get newsletters from your favourite retailers, follow them on social media, and frequently visit their websites to see what deals are happening. Pay attention to the flyers and catalogues you encounter in stores or receive in the mail. Occasionally, you'll come across some truly intriguing bargains!

Second, schedule your purchases to coincide with sales. For instance, wait until the best time to buy a product you need if you know a business is paying an alluring price. You'll save a ton of money by doing this.

Thirdly, keep an eye out for deals on loyalty. Based on your purchases, store and brand loyalty programs may give you unique advantages, gifts, or discounts. To optimize your savings, don't be reluctant to join and use these programs.

Additionally, comparing costs across various retailers and internet retailers is smart. Even after accounting for promotions, you can discover that certain things are more affordable elsewhere. To simplify your work, use specialized apps and price comparison websites. There's no reason to do this with the rest of our spending when we already do it with plane tickets for our vacations. To be clear, I'm not advocating that you spend three hours comparing the prices of carrots at every local supermarket; rather, you should only do this sparingly and sensibly.

Remember to include cashback apps, online shopping clubs, and private sales websites. With the help of these platforms, you may save a significant amount of money, take advantage of special discounts, and receive cashback on some of your purchases.

Lastly, remember that although taking advantage of sales and promotions is a good idea, avoid making impulsive purchases. Purchase only the items you had intended to or truly need. Spending too much should be avoided, even if the offer sounds alluring. Remain mindful of your financial objectives and modify your spending plan as necessary.

Without exceeding your budget, follow these recommendations. You won't have to relinquish life's pleasures to reach your financial objectives and create significant savings.

Invest in your learning and growth as a person.

Go for Official Education:

Enroll in classes, programs, or degrees corresponding to your interests and career objectives.

Think about conventional educational settings, virtual learning environments, or career-training initiatives.

Participate in conferences, seminars, and workshops:

Take part in conferences, seminars, and workshops relevant to your interest.

Attending these events offers the chance to network with professionals, pick the brains of industry experts, and remain current with industry trends.

Look for Certifications in Your Field:

Examine professional qualifications or certificates for your preferred field or career path.

These credentials can improve your marketability and serve as proof of your knowledge.

Take Part in Ongoing Education:

Adopt a perpetual learning mindset and commit to learning new things every day of your work.

To keep up with the most recent advancements in your profession, read books, articles, and trade magazines.

Acquire New Proficiencies:

Determine which abilities are valuable or in demand in your field.

By enrolling in classes, workshops, or online tutorials.

Look for coaches and mentors:

Seek mentors or coaches who, through their knowledge and experiences, may offer direction, encouragement, and insights.

Gain insight from their experience and use their counsel to guide your professional and personal development.

Participate in Professional Associations:

Join organizations or professional groups in your area of expertise.

These communities provide resources, learning opportunities, and networking opportunities to aid your development.

Participate in online courses and webinars:

Benefit from online courses, webinars, and virtual workshops from respectable organizations or professionals.

These platforms make it easy and flexible to learn at your speed.

Taking Part in Activities That Develop Skills:

Take part in side projects, freelancing, or voluntary work that will let you put your skills to use.

These encounters can broaden your professional network and present possibilities for hands-on learning.

Encourage Individual Development

Invest in self-improvement endeavours that improve your mental state, social abilities, and overall well-being.

This can involve leadership development programs, mindfulness exercises, or one-on-one mentoring.

Keep Up with Industry Trends:

Use internet resources, networking, and research to stay current on developments, industry trends, and emerging technology.

Understanding your sector's present and future state is essential for both professional and personal development.

Set Objectives and Monitor Results:

Establish quantifiable, explicit goals for your learning and growth.

Evaluate your progress regularly, make any necessary adjustments to your plans, and acknowledge your accomplishments as you go.

By investing in your education and personal development, you can improve your knowledge, abilities, and competencies and increase your value to clients, companies, and business endeavours. Your ongoing learning and personal development influence your job advancement, general life satisfaction, and professional success.

To summarize, the process of investing in your education and personal growth includes going to conferences and workshops, getting professional certifications, learning continuously, picking up new skills, finding mentors and coaches, joining associations for your industry, taking webinars and online courses, participating in skill-building activities, encouraging personal growth, keeping up with industry trends, setting goals, and monitoring your progress. By prioritizing your development, you invest in your future and provide yourself with the skills and information required to succeed in your chosen field of work or entrepreneurial pursuits.

Investing is a key component of money management.

Making money work for you is even more important than learning how to handle it. An essential component of creating long-term wealth is investing.

Investing is one of the best methods to manage money and may yield incredible profits over an extended period. As you increase your annual investment, your money will be able to expand gradually.

Retirement inverts with an eye toward the long term.

The largest determinant of your comfort level when it comes time to get off the work treadmill is how much you can save for retirement. However, there's also a big impact on how you invest the cash in your retirement accounts. How much you want to invest in stocks and how much in bonds is how you save for retirement. As if I needed to remind you, stocks can sometimes be volatile, but historically, over ten years or more, they have outperformed bonds in terms of returns.

Relationships are more relaxed. They usually rise when stocks rise, not decrease like equities during bad times. They don't, however, make as much money as stocks do. Inflation is a hidden risk when choosing your stock and bond allocation. That's the annoying reality that prices increase with time. In 25 years, a $1,000 purchase will cost more than $1,600, even at a moderate 2% inflation rate. The greatest inflation-beating returns have come from stocks over extended periods.

Your time horizon, the number of years you plan to hold your investments, personal goals, and risk tolerance will determine the best stock-bond ratio. Jack Bogle, the famous Vanguard founder and unwavering champion of individual investors, offered this straightforward rule of thumb: Deduct your age from 110. That is the approximate percentage that you may wish to have on hand.

Invest frequently and early in your future.

When it comes to retirement savings, investing $5,000 year in your 20s earns you twice as much as investing $20,000 annually in your 40s. This is because little amounts of money eventually attract interest. This interest multiplies your money quickly because it also accrues interest. To cut a long tale short, conserving money.

Build a diversified investing portfolio.

Our savings in a bank account will probably be less valuable over time. Savings account interest rates are too low to keep up with inflation. Investing is what financial guru Matthew Blume suggests doing to deal with this. In "Making Smart Investments: A Beginner's Guide," he believes that investing enables one to stay up with inflation-driven rises in the cost of living. At most, compound interest—or growth gained on growth—is the main advantage of a long-term investing strategy.

How do you make investments? For efficient money management, Blume suggests diversifying your investments. Some examples are real estate, commodities, precious metals, venture capital, private equity, and stocks. By preventing all of your assets from being concentrated in one place, diversification aids in risk management. According to Blume, a well-constructed portfolio ought to have a variety of assets (stocks, bonds, etc.) that move in diverse directions from one another. As a result, a portfolio's volatility is decreased without necessarily decreasing its potential return.

Step Number Five

Steer clear of debt.

Although borrowing money to fulfil your dreams is popular, there are drawbacks to using loans for financial purposes. The high interest rate may reduce your funds. Having several loans also lowers your credit score, making it more difficult to get credit when you need it or, in certain situations, even a job. Thus, make every effort to keep your debt to a minimum. Using credit cards excessively or becoming overly indebted might make it difficult to stick to your budget and financially burdensome.

Make a strategy to pay off debt.

One major financial stress is debt. It impacts not just your present spending plan but also your future savings. As you ask yourself, "How can I manage my money properly?" take your debt seriously and make it a priority to pay it off. Consider several debt repayment schemes and select the one that best suits your needs. Keep debt out of the way so you can achieve your financial objectives. To start reducing your debt right now, make a plan. Eliminating debt may also aid in improved money management and decreased money-related anxiety.

The CFPB suggests the following two plans for paying off debt:

The snowball approach aims to pay off your lowest amounts first. You continue to pay the bare minimum toward all of your obligations. Any additional funds are utilized to settle your lowest balance simultaneously. Next, you pay down your next-smallest balance with the money you've freed up, and so on. This could result in lengthier repayment terms for debts with higher interest rates. And in the long run, that can end up costing you more.

Debt avalanche approach: Also known as the highest interest rate method, this technique involves listing your debts in order of interest rate, starting with the highest and working your way down. Your initial payment is made on the debt with the highest interest rate. After that is settled, you can utilize the remaining money to settle the next loan on your list. Additionally, you still only make the minimum payments on all your bills.

You'll feel better mentally when you manage and pay off your debt, and your stress level will decrease as you progress toward payback.

Chapter 6: The Value of Setting Spending Priorities

Do you have ongoing difficulties making ends meet? Are you sick and weary of not having enough money saved for the future and living paycheck to paycheck? Setting spending priorities will help you attain your financial objectives and regain control over your money.

This chapter will discuss the value of spending money in a prioritized manner, how to choose your priorities, and how to maximize your financial resources.

The Significance of Setting Spending Priorities

Putting the most important things to you first when it comes to spending is known as prioritizing. This enables you to allocate your money resources to the pursuits that will maximize your happiness and contentment. Setting expenditure priorities is important for the following reasons:

Reaching Your Financial Objectives

Setting spending priorities will enable you to reach your financial objectives more quickly. You may achieve your objectives more quickly by allocating funds to your top priorities.

You can prioritize your spending by setting aside a certain amount each month, for example, if you are saving for a down payment on a home. To ensure you have adequate money to reach your objectives, you can also reduce wasteful spending on things like eating out or shopping for new clothes.

Having a Happier Life

You will feel more content and happy when you use your money on the most important things. Setting spending priorities will benefit your general well-being, happiness, and ability to cope with stress.

Make travel a priority in your budget, for instance, if you like. While saving money and making travel plans might build excitement and anticipation, the trip can bring happiness and enduring memories. On the other hand, you can experience the same happiness if you make attending concerts a priority.

Making Your Life More Meaningful

You are investing in the things that are most important to you when you set spending priorities. When you accomplish this, you're building a happier, more fulfilling life that aligns with your ideals.

You're investing in important causes, for example, if you volunteer or donate to charities first. This can give you a sense of contentment and purpose that comes with not having to spend money on material possessions.

Setting Priorities

Setting spending priorities starts with determining your priorities. Take these actions to achieve that:

Establish Your Principles

Establish your basic values first. What in life do you value most? What goals do you have in mind? Your values will direct you toward the priorities in your life.

Establish Your Financial Objectives

Set your financial objectives next. What financial goals do you have? Which would you prefer: paying off debt or saving for a down payment on a home? Prioritizing your expenditures will be made easier if you have certain financial goals.

You can begin by making investments in a retirement account if saving for retirement is one of your financial objectives. By doing this, you can ensure that your money is going toward the most important things to you and stay on track with your long-term financial goals.

Review Your Expenses

Examine your present spending patterns carefully. Are you spending money on items supporting your objectives and core beliefs? Or are you squandering cash on items that you don't find important? Assessing your spending patterns will assist you in determining areas in which adjustments are possible.

For example, you may find that you're eating out a lot or subscribing to subscriptions you rarely use. After you've determined these areas, you can make savings and budget your money for items that support your objectives and values.

Maximizing Your Financial Resources

It's time to maximize your financial resources when you've determined your priorities. Here are some pointers to assist you in doing that:

Establish a Budget

When it comes to setting spending priorities, making a budget is crucial. All a budget is is a plan for your financial expenditures. It ensures your money is going toward the things most important to you and helps you track where it is going.

The first step in budgeting is figuring out your income and expenses. Next, order your spending according to your objectives and ideals. This can assist you in identifying areas where you may be overpaying and making savings.

Reduce Superfluous Expenses

Reducing wasteful spending is a terrific method to maximize your financial resources. This doesn't mean you must give up everything you love; instead, figure out how to cut costs without compromising priorities.

If you enjoy dining out, for example, you can continue to do so, but only once a week. You can still enjoy eating out without going over budget in this way. Additionally, you can search for ways to cut costs on entertainment and groceries by using coupons or taking advantage of sales.

Pay Using Cash Rather Than Credit

You can control your spending more easily if you pay with cash instead of credit. Experiencing the physical removal of cash from your wallet can increase your awareness of purchasing habits.

Put Your Savings in Motion

Investing your money wisely can be achieved by automating your savings. You may ensure you're saving a certain amount each month by setting. By doing this, you can ensure that your money is going toward the most important things to you and accelerate the achievement of your financial goals.

Keep an eye on your expenses.

Setting spending priorities requires careful monitoring of your expenditures. You can ensure you're sticking to your spending plan and allocating your funds to your top priorities by keeping track of your expenditures.

You can simply maintain an expense record in a notebook or utilize apps or spreadsheets to track your spending. Regardless of your approach, check your expenditures frequently and make any necessary adjustments to your budget.

In summary

Setting spending priorities is essential to reaching your financial objectives and leading a more contented, joyful life. You can gain financial independence by taking charge of your finances, setting priorities, making the most of your income, and budgeting.

Recall that you don't have to give up everything you enjoy to prioritize your expenditures. Instead, it's about figuring out how to continue to enjoy the things you love and allocate your finances to the most important things. By doing this, you may build a life that fulfils you and is consistent with your ideals.

Observing your repeated "I" statements, like "I'll never make enough money," will reveal a lot about your financial status.

4. Make Just One Modification outside of the body. By purposefully altering a minor behaviour and paying attention to your inner responses, you might learn to adapt to new financial behaviours. Here are a few possible results:

Place your toothbrush in a different location.

- Select a new street to go to a location you frequently visit.
- Lie in bed a little later or rise earlier than normal.
- Switch the news channel.
- Invest in a magazine that you haven't previously seen.
- Replace one serve of ice cream or cake with a healthy snack.
- Go to the meeting you've been thinking about attending.

- Invert the toilet paper roll in your restroom. Practice the new action until you are comfortable doing it. Watch for any signs of disorientation and how long you can become used to the overall change.

Some people feel pain for a few days, while others could endure it for several weeks.

Once you have established your pace and started more new habits, you can predict fairly accurately how long the risks and moving stupids will endure. 5. Modify One Financial Practice. Look at your financial management practices to prepare for financial progress. Here are a few possible results:

- Maintain a continuous tabulation of your daily income and expenses.
- Make on-time weekly bill payments.
- Quit using the credit card that you prefer. Save the cash you would have spent, even if it's only $3 a week.
- Give out some small cash.

- Spend a day living frugally.

Remember your feelings and record them in your prosperity journal when you modify this. For the time being, note down any discomfort you are feeling.

6. Keep an eye out for any resistance to changing your finances.

If you had trouble completing the previous step, consider the following:

- Will my self-perception change if my financial status changes?

- If I am financially successful, what will I worry will happen? Will my identity change if I have financial security? Will my interactions with my family change as a result? Would wealth entail the betrayal of a friend or perhaps a member of one's family?

7. Make a statement

The subconscious mind adopts and uses these ideas to get the intended effects. If you tell your subconscious mind that life is full of opportunity, it will bring opportunities to you; if you tell it that you never get what you want, it will do the opposite.

On the other hand, conflicting beliefs and resistance to change can result in disruption.

For example, it makes no difference how often I tell my subconscious mind that I have an easy cash flow if I also believe, in opposition to that, that it is hard for me to make money.

The same goes for any pain, even dread; I might experience due to easy financial flow.

Managing Debt: Definition and Handling

You have debt if you take out a loan from someone or a business. You must pay back the money you owe, sometimes in set instalments.

You usually use the money from your next salary to make those payments.

Even though you could be able to get anything right away with a loan, you can be stuck with monthly payments for a few months or even a few years.

Debt is not the same as credit. Credit can be obtained even if you have no debt. For example, you may have a credit card that is completely paid off.

Let's discuss managing negative emotions without going bankrupt and emotional spending.

Emotional spending is using money to purchase things to alleviate unpleasant feelings such as stress, melancholy, or boredom. Spending close to home can lead to reckless purchases and overspending, which might result in debt. For example, you could treat yourself to a new device or wardrobe to help you relax after a demanding workday.

Managing emotional spending may be easier by discovering healthier coping mechanisms for unpleasant feelings, such as physical activity, meditation, or quality time spent with loved ones. Practice self-care and introspection to become more aware of your triggers close to home and develop better habits. Finally, try not to engage in buying or shopping as a way to distract yourself from depressing thoughts. Instead, focus on finding solutions to the underlying problems.

www.ingramcontent.com/pod-product-compliance
Lightning Source LLC
Chambersburg PA
CBHW052149110526
44591CB00012B/1917